Report to Congressional Committees

I0425902

May 2012

STATE PARTNERSHIP PROGRAM

Improved Oversight, Guidance, and Training Needed for National Guard's Efforts with Foreign Partners

G A O
Accountability ★ Integrity ★ Reliability

GAO-12-548

STATE PARTNERSHIP PROGRAM

Improved Oversight, Guidance, and Training Needed for National Guard's Efforts with Foreign Partners

G A O
Accountability * Integrity * Reliability

Highlights

Highlights of GAO-12-548, a report to congressional committees

Why GAO Did This Study

The National Guard's State Partnership Program is a DOD security cooperation program that matches state National Guards with foreign countries to conduct joint activities— including visits between senior military leaders and knowledge sharing in areas such as disaster management— that further U.S. national security goals. The program has partnerships between 52 U.S. state and territory National Guards and 69 countries. In fiscal year 2011, program expenditures were at least $13.2 million. The 2012 National Defense Authorization Act directed GAO to study the program. GAO determined (1) the extent to which State Partnership Program activities are meeting program goals and objectives; (2) the types and frequency of activities and funding levels of the program; and (3) any challenges DOD faces in the program's implementation. GAO collected written responses to questions from State Partnership Program Coordinators at the state level, Bilateral Affairs Officers at the U.S. embassies in the partner nations, and officials at the combatant commands, reviewed documents, and interviewed DOD officials.

What GAO Recommends

GAO recommends that DOD complete its comprehensive oversight framework for the State Partnership Program, develop guidance to achieve reliable data on the program, and issue guidance and conduct additional training on the appropriate use of funding for program activities, including those involving civilians. DOD concurred with all recommendations.

View GAO-12-548. For more information, contact John Pendleton at (202) 512-3489 or pendletonj@gao.gov.

What GAO Found

Many State Partnership Program stakeholders, including State Partnership Program Coordinators, Bilateral Affairs Officers, and combatant command officials, cited benefits to the program, but the program lacks a comprehensive oversight framework that includes clear program goals, objectives, and metrics to measure progress against those goals, which limits the Department of Defense's (DOD) and Congress' ability to assess whether the program is an effective and efficient use of resources. The benefits described by all stakeholders focused on the program's contributions to meeting their specific missions, such as building security relationships, providing experience to guardsmen, and supporting combatant commands' missions. Goals, objectives, and metrics to measure progress are necessary for management oversight, and National Guard Bureau officials told GAO that they recognize the need to update the program's goals and develop metrics and have initiated efforts in these areas. Officials expect completion of these efforts in summer 2012. Until program goals and metrics are implemented, DOD cannot fully assess or adequately oversee the program.

State Partnership Program activity data are incomplete as well as inconsistent and funding data are incomplete for fiscal years 2007 through 2011; therefore GAO cannot provide complete information on the types and frequency of activities or total funding amounts for those years. GAO found that the multiple data systems used to track program activities and funding are not interoperable and users apply varying methods and definitions to guide data inputs. The terminology used to identify activity types is inconsistent across the combatant commands and the National Guard Bureau. Further, funding data from the National Guard Bureau and the combatant commands were incomplete, and while the National Guard Bureau provided its total spending on the program since 2007, it could not provide information on the cost of individual activities. Although the National Guard Bureau has initiated efforts to improve the accuracy of its own State Partnership Program data, without common agreement with the combatant commands on what types of data need to be tracked and how to define activities, the data cannot be easily reconciled across databases.

The most prominent challenge cited by State Partnership Program stakeholders involved how to fund activities that include U.S. and foreign partner civilian participants. Activities involving civilians, for example, have included subject-matter expert exchanges on military support to civil authorities and maritime border security. Although DOD guidance does not prohibit civilian involvement in activities, many stakeholders have the impression that the U.S. military is not permitted to engage civilians in State Partnership Program activities and some states may have chosen not to conduct any events with civilians due to the perception that it may violate DOD guidance. DOD and the National Guard Bureau are working on developing additional guidance and training in this area. Until these efforts are completed, confusion may continue to exist and hinder the program's full potential to fulfill National Guard and combatant command missions.

Contents

United States Government Accountability Office
Washington, DC 20548

May 15, 2012

The Honorable Carl Levin
Chairman
The Honorable John McCain
Ranking Member
Committee on Armed Services
United States Senate

The Honorable Howard P. McKeon
Chairman
The Honorable Adam Smith
Ranking Member
Committee on Armed Services
House of Representatives

The National Guard State Partnership Program—a Department of Defense (DOD) security cooperation program that pairs state National Guards with foreign countries—works to promote national objectives, stability, partner capacity, and better understanding and trust between the United States and foreign countries. The State Partnership Program is one of many efforts within DOD to address security cooperation and its overarching vision is to establish and sustain enduring relationships with partner countries in support of the U.S. national security strategy. The program began in 1993 with 13 partner countries, primarily from the former Soviet Union, to help improve relations with these countries and help reform their defense establishments after the end of the Cold War. Today the program has partnerships between 52 states and territories and 69[1] foreign countries spread throughout the regions of all six

---

[1]There are currently 63 active partnerships. One of those partnerships is between Florida and the U.S. Virgin Islands with the Regional Security System, a collective security agreement for seven island nations in the Eastern Caribbean. The seven nations that participate in the Regional Security System are Antigua and Barbuda, Barbados, Dominica, Grenada, Saints Kitts and Nevis, Saint Lucia, and Saint Vincent and the Grenadines. Two countries, Colombia and Turkmenistan, do not currently have a state National Guard partner assigned.

geographic combatant commands[2] and focuses on building the capacity of and relationships with partner countries' militaries through exchanges of military skills and experience, sharing defense knowledge, enhancing partnership capacity, and furthering mutual security cooperation.

DOD defines State Partnership Program activities as any security cooperation activity supported by funds appropriated to DOD, occurring between a state's National Guard personnel and that state's partner nation, consistent with the State Partnership Program. Activities can vary depending on the needs of the partner nation, the capabilities of the state or territory National Guard, and the priorities of the geographic combatant commander and the U.S. ambassador of the partner country. Through this program, states' National Guard personnel work with their partner countries to conduct activities, such as knowledge sharing from subject matter experts, demonstrations of particular National Guard capabilities, and visits between senior military leaders, and cover topics such as disaster management, military education, non-commissioned officer development, and border operations. The National Guard Bureau provides guidance to the states participating in the program, but the program is primarily managed by a State Partnership Program Coordinator—a full-time National Guardsman at the state level—and a Bilateral Affairs Officer—normally a full-time National Guardsman or other military officer assigned to the geographic combatant command and under the direction of the U.S. embassy in the partner country.[3] State Partnership Program activities are planned collaboratively by the State Partnership Program Coordinators, the Bilateral Affairs Officers, the U.S. embassy country teams, and the geographic combatant commands.

---

[2]There are six geographic combatant commands: U.S. European Command, U.S. Africa Command, U.S. Pacific Command, U.S. Northern Command, U.S. Southern Command, and U.S. Central Command. There are also three functional combatant commands: U.S. Strategic Command, U.S. Special Operations Command, and U.S. Transportation Command. The functional combatant commands play no role in the State Partnership Program, and throughout this report we refer only to the geographic combatant commands.

[3]Some countries within the U.S. Southern Command use Traditional Commander's Activities coordinators in this role. The combatant commands fund Traditional Commander's Activities coordinators, while the National Guard Bureau funds Bilateral Affairs Officers. For consistency purposes in this report, we refer to all of these personnel as Bilateral Affairs Officers.

According to National Guard Bureau officials, in fiscal year 2008, the National Guard Bureau spent about $2.52 million on the program and in fiscal year 2011 the National Guard Bureau spent about $6.1 million. This money, according to National Guard Bureau officials, provides for the pay and allowances of guardsmen while they are conducting an activity with a partner country and is authorized to be used for military personnel only. Additional money, about $7.1 million in fiscal year 2011, is provided by the combatant commands from a variety of sources, such as Traditional Combatant Commander's Activities funds, Cooperative Threat Reduction Program funds, and Warsaw Initiative Fund/Partnership for Peace funds.

The National Defense Authorization Act for Fiscal Year 2012 directed us to conduct a study of the National Guard State Partnership Program.[4] To meet this mandate, we assessed (1) the extent to which State Partnership Program activities are meeting the goals and objectives of the program; (2) the types and frequency of activities and funding levels associated with the program; and (3) the challenges, if any, that DOD faces in the implementation of the program.

To address these objectives, we obtained perspectives, including views on the benefits of the program, from the Office of the Secretary of Defense for Policy, Joint Staff, National Guard Bureau, and program stakeholders including State Partnership Program coordinating officials at the geographic combatant commands, State Partnership Program Coordinators, and Bilateral Affairs Officers. We also collected information on the process that DOD uses to establish partnerships. We requested and analyzed documentation about the goals and objectives of the

---

[4]Section 1234 of the National Defense Authorization Act for Fiscal Year 2012, Pub. L. No. 112-81 (2011), requires us to submit a report to the House and Senate Armed Services Committees on the State Partnership Program that includes: (1) a summary of the sources of funds for the State Partnership Program over the last 5 years; (2) an analysis of the types and frequency of activities performed by participants in the State Partnership Program; (3) a description of the objectives of the State Partnership Program and the manner in which objectives under the program are established and coordinated with the Office of the Secretary of Defense, the geographic combatant commands, United States Country Teams, and other departments and agencies of the United States Government; (4) a description of the manner in which the Department of Defense selects and designates particular State and foreign country partnerships under the State Partnership Program; (5) a description of the manner in which the department measures the effectiveness of the activities under the State Partnership Program in meeting the objectives of the program; and (6) an assessment of the effectiveness of the activities under the State Partnership Program in meeting the objectives of the program.

program and any guidance that would describe how the program is to be implemented. To determine the extent to which State Partnership Program activities are meeting the goals and objectives of the program, we interviewed National Guard Bureau officials about the development of goals, objectives, and performance metrics for the program. We also contacted all State Partnership Program Coordinators and Bilateral Affairs Officers who participate in this program with open-ended questions by e-mail. We collected and analyzed responses from 50 of the 52 State Partnership Program Coordinators and from 23 out of 47 Bilateral Affairs Officers.[5] We also collected and analyzed written responses to similar questions from the coordinating officials at the six U.S. geographic combatant commands. To determine the types and frequency of activities and funding levels associated with the program, we collected and analyzed data on State Partnership Program activities—including types of activities, funding sources, and funding amounts—obtained from the National Guard Bureau and the six U.S. geographic combatant commands from fiscal years 2007 through 2011. To assess the reliability of the data, we collected written information from the combatant commands on their databases. We also discussed the procedures for generating and verifying the data with knowledgeable combatant command and National Guard Bureau officials and, where possible, examined the data for anomalies. We discussed the limitations we identified in the data with the officials, and those limitations are discussed in this report. To identify challenges that DOD faces in implementing the program, we included relevant questions when we contacted all State Partnership Program Coordinators and all Bilateral Affairs Officers who participate in this program, and the six U.S. geographic combatant commands, as described above. We conducted this performance audit from August 2011 to May 2012 in accordance with generally accepted government auditing standards. Those standards require that we plan and perform the audit to obtain sufficient, appropriate evidence to provide a reasonable basis for our findings and conclusions based on our audit objectives. We believe that the evidence obtained provides a reasonable basis for our findings and conclusions based on our audit objectives. A more detailed description of our scope and methodology is included in appendix I.

---

[5]There are 52 states and territories currently participating in the State Partnership Program. While there are 63 partnerships in the program, not every country has a Bilateral Affairs Officer assigned.

Background

The State Partnership Program grew from the former Joint Contact Team Program, a program comprised of active component personnel that sought to establish professional contacts between the U.S. military and the militaries of newly independent nations of the former Soviet Union. The Joint Contact Team Program was intended to promote subordination to civilian leadership, respect for human rights, and a defensively oriented military posture. In 1993, the National Guard Bureau was integrated into the Joint Contact Team Program to initiate the first state partnerships, as it was believed that Russia would find the National Guard less provocative than a U.S. active duty full-time military presence. The program has since expanded to 63 partnerships covering all combatant commands, with nearly all state National Guards participating. Figure 1 illustrates the number of partner country relationships within each combatant command.

Figure 1: State Partnership Program Participating States and Countries, by Combatant Command

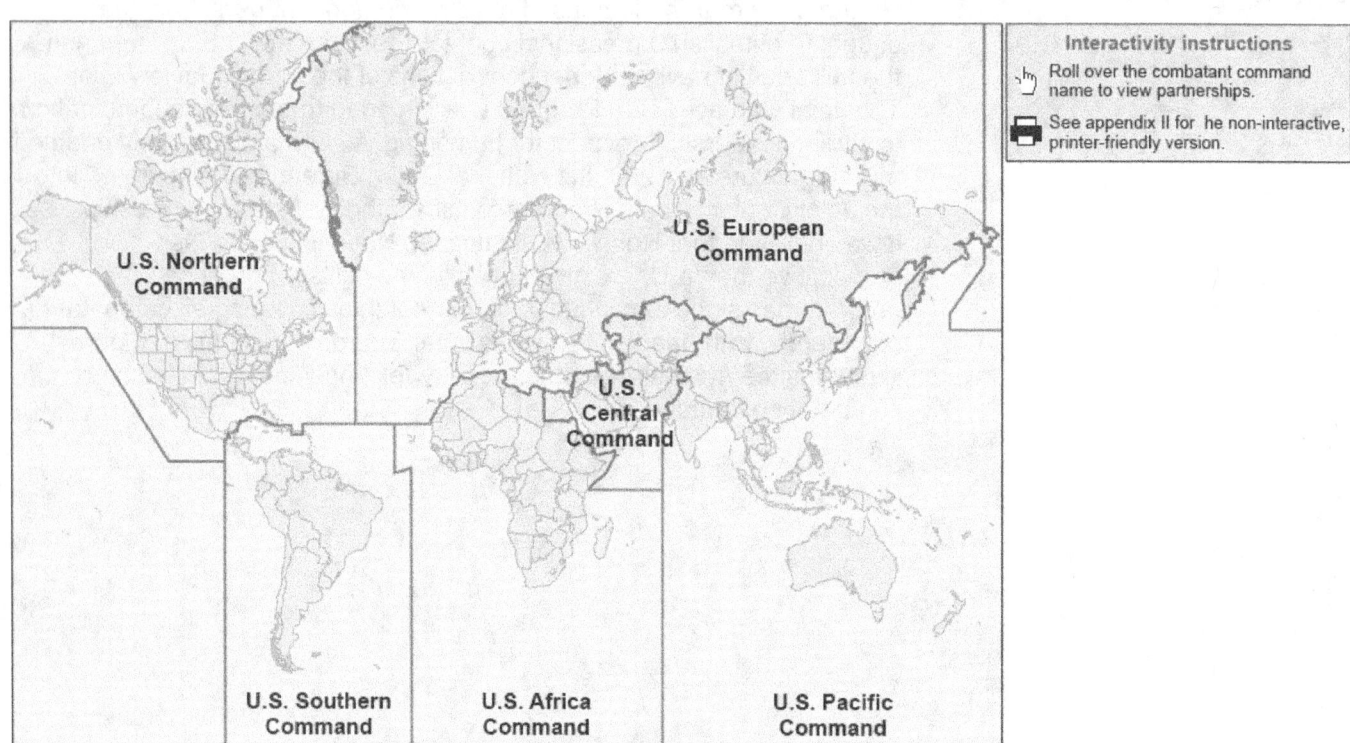

Source: National Guard Bureau.

*Indicates country has a Bilateral Affairs Officer.

Both the 2010 *Quadrennial Defense Review Report* and the 2011 *National Military Strategy of the United States of America* identify security cooperation and building partner capacity as priorities in multiple regions, including the Middle East, Africa, and Asia. In addition, both documents emphasize the need to strengthen and expand the United States' network of international partnerships to enhance security, and the National Military Strategy instructs the combatant commands, among others, to partner with other agencies to pursue theater security cooperation. As such, the State Partnership Program acts as a force enabler for the combatant commands, and State Partnership Program activities are part of the combatant commands' theater security cooperation plans. State Partnership Program activities are to be approved by the combatant commands, as well as the U.S. ambassador in their respective partner nations, before they can be executed.

Any nation requesting a state partnership sends its official request to its respective U.S. ambassador. Once the partnership is endorsed, the request is forwarded to the appropriate combatant command. If the combatant command finds that the partnership meets strategic objectives and priorities, the combatant command sends the request to the National Guard Bureau. The Chief of the National Guard Bureau reviews the request to determine the viability of the partnership. If the Chief accepts the request, he or she notifies the combatant command and solicits proposals from the adjutants general of the state Guards. State Guard proposals include a statement of intent; background on the state Guard and its capabilities; proposed areas of military engagement with the partner nation; potential benefits to both the state Guard and partner nation; discussion of historical, cultural, and academic similarities between the state and the partner nation; and any documentation supporting the state Guard's nomination. The proposals go through three levels of review within DOD, and the Chief of the National Guard Bureau forwards a recommended nominee to the combatant command and the partner country's U.S. embassy for final approval. Figure 2 illustrates the request and approval process.

Figure 2: Process for Establishing New Partnerships

Requesting nation	U.S. embassy	Combatant Command	National Guard Bureau	Combatant Command	U.S. embassy	Requesting nation
Formally requests state partnership with letter to ambassador	Endorses partnership concept	Confirms Guidance for Employment of the Force, functional, regional priorities	Provides intragency and interagency coordination	Coordinates with U.S. embassy team	Endorses partner selection	Partnership activities begin
			Evaluates state applications, provides partner recommendation		Notifies requesting country	

Source: GAO analysis of National Guard Bureau information.

State Partnership Program Stakeholders Cited Benefits but Program Oversight Is Hindered by Lack of Clear Goals, Objectives, and Progress Measures

State Partnership Program stakeholders, including State Partnership Program Coordinators, Bilateral Affairs Officers, and combatant command officials, cited benefits of the program, but the program lacks clear goals, objectives, and performance metrics. Without a comprehensive oversight framework for defining and measuring progress, DOD cannot fully assess whether the program is an effective and efficient use of resources.

Stakeholders Cited Benefits of the State Partnership Program

State Partnership Program Coordinators provided examples of how the program benefits their states and their National Guard units, including providing experience and training for guardsmen and developing relationships between the state and the partner country. For example, 39 of the 50 State Partnership Program Coordinators who responded to our questions reported that the State Partnership Program provides experience to participating guardsmen. In another instance, one State Partnership Program Coordinator reported that by demonstrating medical techniques to partner country participants, the guardsmen simultaneously gain direct experience performing those techniques. Three State Partnership Program Coordinators specifically noted that the program allows participants to deploy and complete realistic military training outside a warzone. In addition, 17 State Partnership Program Coordinators noted the value of the State Partnership Program in providing a mechanism for developing relationships between the state Guard units and the partner countries. Another State Partnership

Program Coordinator noted that establishing such relationships improves long-term international security, and several State Partnership Program Coordinators noted that the relationships fostered by the program were instrumental in the partner countries' deployments to Afghanistan or Iraq.

All six combatant commands and all 23 Bilateral Affairs Officers who responded to our questions reported that the State Partnership Program supports their missions and objectives, including promoting stability and security cooperation and assisting with building partner capacity. For example, one Bilateral Affairs Officer reported that a State Partnership Program activity on women's leadership in the military met the geographic combatant command's objective of building partner capacity, as well as U.S. country team objectives to advance human rights, advance public diplomacy, and strengthen regional security capabilities. The activity covered deployment preparations, leadership development, and sexual assault prevention. Three of the six combatant commands specifically noted that the National Guard units are uniquely suited to assist the combatant command in building the capacity of partner countries as a result of their civilian and military experiences. For example, in one combatant command, State Partnership Program activities were used to support combatant command objectives by providing subject matter expertise to Royal Bahamas Police Force Drug Enforcement Unit officers in the field of combat trauma care. Thirteen Bilateral Affairs Officers also cited the benefit of the State Partnership Program's ability to develop and maintain relationships between the state Guard units and the partner countries. For example, one Bilateral Affairs Officer stated that the relationship between one state Guard unit and its partner country was leveraged to assist the country in making progress toward the country team's goal of anchoring the country in European and Euro-Atlantic institutions. The partner country was originally reluctant to accept assistance with military personnel management due to cultural sensitivities, but based on the established relationship, the state Guard unit was granted full access and made suggestions that were implemented by the partner country. Table 1 summarizes the key benefits of the program as described by State Partnership Program Coordinators, Bilateral Affairs Officers, and officials from the combatant commands.

Table 1: Key Benefits of the State Partnership Program, as Cited by State Partnership Program Coordinators, Bilateral Affairs Officers, and Officials from Combatant Commands

State Partnership Program Coordinators	Bilateral Affairs Officers	Officials from combatant commands
Provides experience and training for guardsmen	Events are tied to combatant command or country team mission	Events support combatant command mission and objectives
Develops relationship with partner country	Good communication and coordination between stakeholders	National Guard units possess unique skills that are useful for supporting combatant command objectives
Encourages partner countries to co-deploy to Iraq or Afghanistan	Provides information sharing and support to partner country	Encourages partner nation deployment to Iraq or Afghanistan
Improves retention or provides other incentives for guardsmen	Builds relationship with partner country	
Guardsmen benefit from partner country's experiences	Encourages partner countries to co-deploy to Iraq or Afghanistan	

Source: GAO analysis of responses to e-mailed questions.

In addition, European Command's combatant commander testified to Congress in February 2012 that the State Partnership Program develops important strategic relationships that benefit ongoing military activities.[6] The European Command indicated in written responses to our questions that this program helps maintain access to partner countries' leadership and is vital to defense institution building. Similarly, the National Guard Bureau describes the State Partnership Program as fitting within the building partner capacity portfolio of DOD, and views the program as an integral component of DOD's global security cooperation strategy that can contribute to enhanced security. Further, it sees the program as integral to the combatant commands' theater engagement plans and the U.S. Ambassadors' Mission Strategic Resource Plans. Moreover, the National Guard Bureau told us that it found that the State Partnership Program is valuable to U.S. ambassadors. In October 2010, the National Guard Bureau, in conjunction with the Department of State, surveyed the ambassadors of U.S. embassies with State Partnership Program partnerships as part of an effort to conduct a strategic review of the program. Forty-one of the 62 ambassadors surveyed provided responses, and 40 of the respondents agreed that the State Partnership Program is a valuable tool in advancing their mission goals and objectives.

---

[6]*Fiscal Year 2013 National Defense Authorization Budget Request from U.S. European Command and U.S. Africa Command*, 112th Cong. 16 (2012), statement of Admiral James G. Stavridis, United States Navy Commander, United States European Command before the House Armed Services Committee.

Respondents noted that the activities and relationships developed by the program—fostering activities to support joint military exercises and deployments, providing support for international peacekeeping operations, and embedding training teams—promote overall national security and strategic interests. Thirty-nine ambassadors agreed that there are mechanisms to ensure that activities are properly integrated with U.S. country team priorities.

The State Partnership Program Does Not Have Agreed-Upon Goals or Metrics to Assess Progress

Despite considerable anecdotal evidence from many State Partnership Program stakeholders about the program's benefits, we were unable to comprehensively assess the State Partnership Program because the National Guard Bureau has not updated its program goals or objectives to match the program's current operations. The National Guard Bureau developed goals and objectives for the program in 2007, but officials told us that these goals and objectives need to be updated to reflect the program as it currently operates. The previous goals and supporting objectives were broadly stated and reflected the desire to build partner capacity, but did little to clarify the specific goals for the State Partnership Program. We have previously reported that achieving results in government requires a comprehensive oversight framework that includes clear goals, measurable objectives, and metrics for assessing progress.[7] Officials stated that they recognize the need to update program goals and objectives to more accurately reflect the current environment and the focus on military-to-military activities, and reported that they have initiated such efforts and expect the new goals and objectives to be finalized by July 2012. Officials also indicated that the new program goals and objectives will be more closely aligned with the combatant commands' strategic goals and objectives.

National Guard Bureau officials also acknowledged that once they update program goals and objectives, they will need to develop metrics to measure results of the program. However, they indicated that due to the relationship-building nature of the program, it is difficult to establish appropriate metrics that capture the effects of the program. As we have previously reported, performance measurement is the ongoing monitoring and reporting of program accomplishments, focused on regularly

---

[7]GAO, *Preventing Sexual Harassment: DOD Needs Greater Leadership Commitment and an Oversight Framework*, GAO-11-809 (Washington, D.C.: Sept. 21, 2011).

collected data on the level and type of program activities, direct products and services delivered by the program, and the results of those activities.[8] As we have previously reported, it is sometimes difficult to establish performance measures for outcomes that are not readily observable and that in those cases, more in-depth program evaluation may be needed in addition to performance measures.[9] Program evaluations are systematic studies conducted periodically that examine programs in-depth and include context in order to examine the extent to which a program is meeting its objectives.[10] The RAND Corporation, a nonpartisan nonprofit organization that conducts public policy research, has reported on performance measures that programs like the State Partnership Program, which engage in building partner capacity and other security cooperation activities, can use to demonstrate results.[11] Further, other federal agencies engaged in security cooperation activities use program evaluations in addition to performance measures. For example, the United States Agency for International Development has implemented multiple program evaluations for its foreign assistance programs, and the Global Peace Operations Initiative within the Department of State uses program evaluations to gauge the effectiveness of its training programs. National Guard Bureau officials told us that they are working with experts from other organizations including RAND and the Defense Security Cooperation Agency and have begun to develop metrics for the program. They provided us with a draft document containing some key assessment indicators in the areas of operational and mission support, doctrine and training, and systemic support. Under the area of mission support, for

---

[8]GAO, *Performance Measurement and Evaluation: Definitions and Relationships,* GAO-11-646SP (Washington, D.C.: May 2011).

[9]GAO, *Results-Oriented Government: GPRA Has Established a Solid Foundation for Achieving Greater Results,* GAO-04-38 (Washington, D.C.: Mar. 10, 2004) and GAO-11-646SP.

[10]GAO-11-646SP.

[11]RAND, *Developing an Army Strategy for Building Partner Capacity for Stability Operations* (2010). In this report, RAND lists generic indicators used as a basis for measuring the effectiveness of various types of security cooperation programs in meeting the objective of establishing a safe and secure environment in the partner nation. See also RAND, *Prototype Handbook for Monitoring and Evaluating Department of Defense Humanitarian Assistance Projects* (2011). In this handbook, RAND provides guidance, analytic tools, and measures to demonstrate the effectiveness of humanitarian assistance projects, which also are intended to build upon nations' capacities; and show how those projects link to strategic-level goals, including those of the country teams and combatant commands.

example, officials stated they are planning to track how effective State Partnership Program activities are in meeting combatant command and country team priorities. Officials further stated that these metrics are expected to be finalized during the summer of 2012. Such goals and metrics would form the foundation for a comprehensive oversight framework and, until they are put into place, DOD cannot fully assess whether the program is an effective and efficient use of resources.

Complete Information about Activities and Funding Is Unavailable

We cannot provide complete information on the types and frequency of State Partnership Program activities or the total funding amounts for these activities for fiscal years 2007 to 2011 because activity data are incomplete as well as inconsistent and funding data are incomplete. According to *Standards for Internal Control in the Federal Government*, program managers and decision makers should have reliable data to determine whether they are meeting goals and using resources effectively and efficiently.[12] Without complete and consistent data on the State Partnership Program, we and DOD cannot assess the program's efficiency nor provide complete information to decision makers, including Congress.

Data on State Partnership Program Activities Are Incomplete and Inconsistent

Data on State Partnership Program activities from the combatant commands and the National Guard Bureau are incomplete and inconsistent. The National Guard Bureau and the combatant commands maintain separate databases for tracking events. Each entity independently tracks its activities and funding in databases that are not interoperable. According to National Guard Bureau officials, DOD's *Guidance for Employment of the Force* mandates that all security cooperation activities be tracked, including State Partnership Program activities, in management information system databases. The National Guard Bureau uses its own system to track State Partnership Program events that it funds. National Guard Bureau officials indicated that events funded by a combatant command and the National Guard Bureau would

---

[12]GAO, *Standards for Internal Control in the Federal Government,* GAO/AIMD-00-21.3.1 (Washington, D.C.: Nov. 1999).

be tracked in both databases.[13] National Guard Bureau officials told us that as a result, data must be pulled from both the combatant commands' and the National Guard Bureau's data systems to glean the most complete information on the funding of State Partnership Program activities.

We asked the combatant commands and the National Guard Bureau to provide us with a list of all State Partnership Program activities since fiscal year 2007, but the data that they provided to us were incomplete. Africa Command could only provide data since fiscal year 2009, when the command became fully operational, but officials told us that it is possible not all State Partnership Program activities are included in the data it provided because there is no way to electronically search for State Partnership Program activities in its database since they are not annotated as State Partnership Program activities. According to an Africa Command official, the data provided were selected manually, and some activities may have been overlooked. Activity data provided to us by European Command were also incomplete in that the location of events was missing for 482 of 753 (64 percent) activities. European Command officials told us that while the database does not always contain information on the location of events, individual records, such as after-action reviews for specific events, would have this information. In addition, the National Guard Bureau data were missing for fiscal year 2009 because the data system was not yet operational and data were not centrally maintained. National Guard Bureau officials told us that data were incomplete for 2010 because it was the first year that the National Guard Bureau began to use this data system to collect State Partnership Program data and staff had to learn how to use the system.

Further, we found that some activity information that should have been contained in both combatant command and National Guard Bureau databases was not. For example, Northern Command and Pacific Command reported that a majority of State Partnership Program activities in their areas of responsibility were funded by the National Guard Bureau. As a result, we expected that the activity data would be maintained in both the combatant commands' and the National Guard Bureau's

---

[13]The combatant commands use several types of databases to maintain their information. Several of the combatant commands use the Theater Security Cooperation Management Information System. The National Guard Bureau currently uses the Army Global Outlook System as its database for maintaining information on the State Partnership Program.

databases. However, when we compared the data provided by the combatant commands, including Northern Command, to the data provided by the National Guard Bureau, we found that both had records of State Partnership Program activities that were not accounted for in the other's database. In addition, we compared a sample of the data provided to us by the combatant commanders and the National Guard Bureau to the activities listed in a DOD report to Congress on a subset of State Partnership Program activities involving civilians.[14] Our analysis showed that 32 activities in the report to Congress were not accounted for in the data provided to us, despite the broader scope of our data request. The National Guard Bureau officials told us that their database was not used to meet the data request for the DOD report because they don't have data from the required years. Instead, individual state Guard units were asked through a data call from the National Guard Bureau to provide lists of activities.

Through our data analysis, we also found that activities in the National Guard Bureau and the combatant command databases were inconsistently defined, which hindered our ability to report on the types and frequency of activities. The combatant commands and the National Guard Bureau reported a broad range of activities conducted for fiscal years 2007 through 2011, but common activities included knowledge sharing on an area of expertise by National Guard personnel with partner nation participants, demonstrations of National Guard capabilities, and visits between an adjutant general or other high ranking U.S. military official with senior leaders of the partner nation's armed forces. However, the terminology used to identify activity types varied both across the combatant commands and between the combatant commands and the National Guard Bureau. An August 2011 Directive Type Memorandum from the Under Secretary of Defense for Policy provides a definition for a State Partnership Program activity, but it does not define specific activity types.[15] We found that the combatant commands use different terms to

---

[14]Department of Defense, *State Partnership Program Fiscal Years 2009 & 2011* (Dec. 2011).

[15]Under Secretary of Defense for Policy Memorandum, *Directive-Type Memorandum (DTM) 11-010, "Use of Appropriated Funds for Conducting State Partnership Program (SPP) Activities"* (Aug. 19, 2011). According to the Directive Type Memorandum, a State Partnership Program activity is any security cooperation activity supported by funds appropriated to DOD, occurring between a State's National Guard personnel and the partner country, consistent with the State Partnership Program.

GAO-12-548 State Partnership Program

define similar activities. For example, one combatant command used the term orientation to describe the partner country observances of U.S. forces in action, whereas another combatant command referred to those activities as familiarizations. The user's manual for the National Guard Bureau's database contains a list of different activity types, but the types themselves are not consistent with the terminology used by the combatant commands. For example, in their respective databases, the National Guard Bureau used the term military-to-military for most of its activities that involve U.S. military activities conducted with host country militaries, whereas the combatant commands used terms like familiarization or traveling contact team, making it difficult to identify if the data in different databases were describing the same activity or two separate activities.[16] In addition, although State Partnership Program activities that are funded by both a combatant command and the National Guard Bureau should be entered into each entity's database for its respective funded amount, four combatant commands and the National Guard Bureau reported that there is no standard method for all the combatant commands and the National Guard Bureau to ensure the separate entries can be easily compiled in order to see all data maintained on a particular activity, including the total funding amount of the activity. Because of these inconsistencies, we could not summarize the types or frequency of activities that have taken place under the State Partnership Program.

State Partnership Program Funding Information Is Incomplete

The funding data for State Partnership Program activities from fiscal years 2007 through 2011 are incomplete, thus preventing us from providing complete information on the total cost of the program. As previously discussed, funding data on State Partnership Program activities are maintained in multiple databases, depending primarily on the funding source for the activity. We found that funding data from the National Guard Bureau and some of the combatant commands were incomplete. For example, National Guard Bureau officials told us that that there was no standardized method for collecting and centrally managing its own State Partnership Program data prior to fiscal year 2009, when

---

[16]Other terms for activity types used in the National Guard Bureau's database include seminar/workshop, bilateral conference, senior official visit, and subject matter expert exchange, among others. The combatant commands use a variety of terms for activity types, including subject matter expert exchange, exchange, senior leadership visit, conference, and assessment.

their database was first implemented. While the National Guard Bureau could tell us the total amount of money it spent on the program since 2007, it could not tell us how much money the National Guard Bureau spent on individual activities. In addition, our analysis also indicated that the funding data maintained by the combatant commands are incomplete, as described below.

- **European Command**: From fiscal years 2007 through 2011, European Command's funding data were missing for 415 out of 753 activities (about 55 percent). European Command officials told us that missing information could indicate that an event had not been executed, that the activity was funded by a source other than the combatant command, or that the information was not updated in the database. Officials stated that business processes were put into place at the end of fiscal year 2010 to prevent this problem from recurring and our analysis showed that data were improved in fiscal year 2011.
- **Africa Command**: For fiscal years 2009 through 2011, Africa Command was missing funding data for 9 out of 70 (about 13 percent) State Partnership Program events. An Africa Command official explained that this could indicate that the event had not yet occurred or had been canceled, or it could indicate that the data were missing.
- **Pacific Command**: Data provided by Pacific Command showed that 118 events took place in its area of responsibility from fiscal years 2007 through 2011, but information on the source of funding for 41 events (about 35 percent) was missing. According to Pacific Command officials, most of the State Partnership Program activities in Pacific Command's area of responsibility were funded by the National Guard Bureau rather than the command. However, for the activities that it did fund, it could only provide projected funding amounts and not expenditure data.[17] According to a Pacific Command official, missing data were most likely due to personnel turnover at the state level.
- **Southern Command**: Data provided by Southern Command were likely complete, but Southern Command officials stated that gathering the data was difficult due to the lack of interoperability of the multiple databases containing the data.

---

[17]Pacific Command provided funding for three events through the Asia Pacific Regional Initiative since fiscal year 2007. The Asia Pacific Regional Initiative is a program designed to build cooperative military relationships with allies in the pacific region.

GAO-12-548 State Partnership Program

- **Central Command**: Data provided by Central Command were also likely complete but officials told us that Central Command's data systems do not always update accurately and therefore officials manually track events on a spreadsheet outside of the database. Data provided to us were based on this spreadsheet, rather than the database.
- **Northern Command**: Officials from Northern Command told us that it did not fund any State Partnership Program events as all events within Northern Command's area of responsibility were funded by the National Guard Bureau.

As a result, funding data for 2007 through 2010 are unavailable due to the incompleteness of the data. Funding data for fiscal year 2011 are the most complete, but the amount presented is only an estimate, as some data are still missing. We found that for fiscal year 2011 the National Guard Bureau and the combatant commands spent at least $13.2 million on State Partnership Program activities. Figure 3 below depicts available expenditure information for fiscal year 2011.

Figure 3: Approximate Expenditures on State Partnership Program Events, Fiscal Year 2011

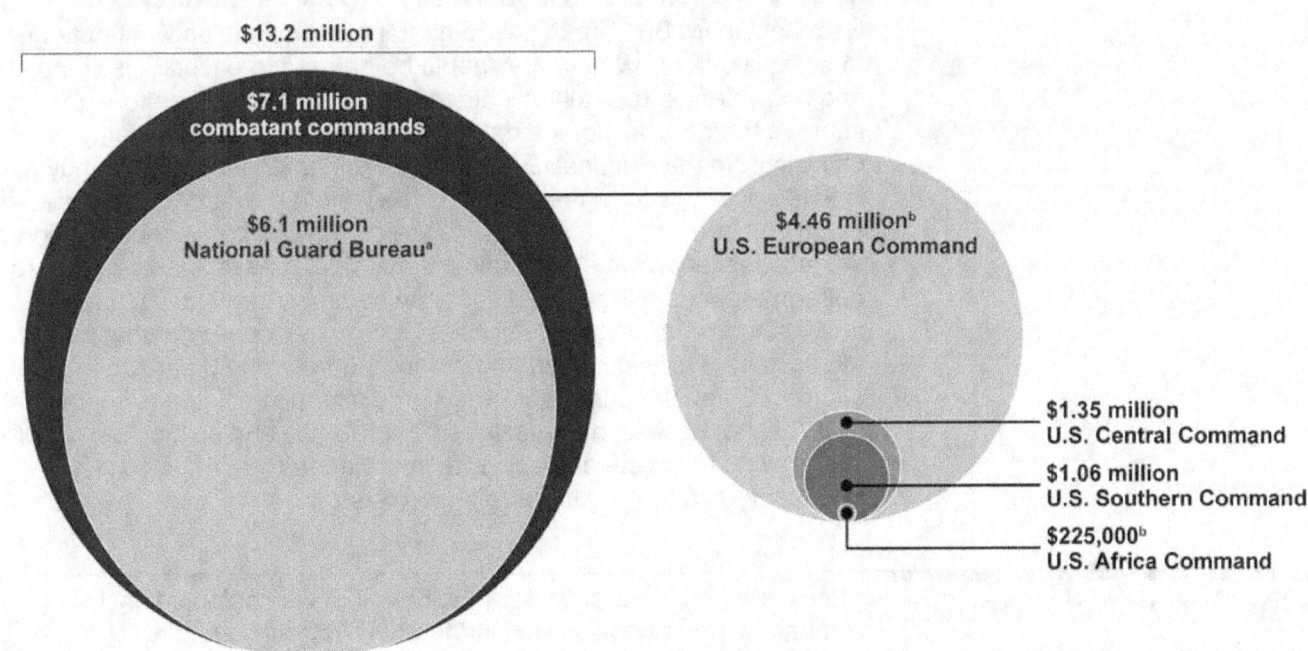

$13.2 million

$7.1 million
combatant commands

$6.1 million
National Guard Bureau[a]

$4.46 million[b]
U.S. European Command

$1.35 million
U.S. Central Command

$1.06 million
U.S. Southern Command

$225,000[b]
U.S. Africa Command

Source: GAO analysis of National Guard Bureau and DOD information.

Note: Funding data presented in this figure are estimates as the data are not complete.

[a]The National Guard Bureau provided total amounts expended per state by year, while the combatant commands provided amounts expended per activity. We totaled these amounts to obtain the amounts shown in this figure.

[b]Data provided by Africa Command and European Command were incomplete.

DOD Lacks Guidance on Current State Partnership Program Data Management

DOD is developing a single global data system, but currently there are no common methods for tracking data on the State Partnership Program or coordinated efforts to address inconsistencies. Specifically, DOD has recognized that multiple databases, operating independently and lacking interoperability, are a problem and is developing a single, global data system—the Global Theater Security Cooperation Management Information System—to replace the multiple databases now being used to capture theater security-type information from various programs, of which the State Partnership Program is one. However, the development of this global data system is still in its early stages and the department does not know when the system is expected to have full operational capabilities. In the absence of a common data system, we found that currently there is no guidance from the Under Secretary of Defense for Policy,[18] the National Guard Bureau, or the combatant commands on what data need to be tracked or how the data should be entered to ensure it is complete and consistent across all the databases, and that current efforts to improve the accuracy of the data are not coordinated. For example, officials from the National Guard Bureau told us that the efforts they have initiated are specific to the database the National Guard Bureau uses and that they have not coordinated with the combatant commands to address the inconsistency issues that occur across databases. Moreover, there is not agreement among stakeholders on common terms to use in describing how to annotate activities in their respective databases so that they can be easily identified and reconciled from one database to another. Given the current inconsistency and incompleteness of the data, DOD cannot assess the program's performance and neither we nor DOD can provide complete and accurate information on activity types, frequency, and funding to decision makers.

Challenges in Funding Activities and Incorporating U.S. and Foreign Partner Civilians Require Additional Guidance and Training

State Partnership Program stakeholders that we contacted, including combatant commands, State Partnership Program Coordinators, and Bilateral Affairs Officers, cited several types of challenges in funding State Partnership Program activities and in incorporating U.S. and foreign partner civilians into events. Specifically, stakeholders cited funding challenges such as concerns about funding availability and funding for events that included civilians. Although guidance and training exist on funding for the program, stakeholders expressed confusion in response to our questions. Until clarifying guidance and training are developed and provided, the National Guard Bureau and the combatant commanders may not be able to fully maximize the State Partnership Program in meeting their missions.

---

[18]According to Directive Type Memorandum 11-010, the Under Secretary of Defense for Policy is the principal adviser to the Secretary of Defense for State Partnership Program policy and programs.

Stakeholders Expressed Concerns about Funding of Activities and Civilian Involvement

When we asked stakeholders a broad, open-ended question about challenges facing the program, funding was a frequently cited problem. Four combatant commands, six Bilateral Affairs Officers, and 20 State Partnership Program Coordinators told us that funding was a challenge to the program. The combatant commands expressed concerns about the availability of funding for the program. For example, one combatant command stated that the most challenging aspect of the State Partnership Program is the funding of the guardsmen because they need to be put on special orders that are not necessary when using active duty personnel. Another combatant command stated that additional funding for the program "is critical for the continued success of the program" as several other countries would like to join the program, and two combatant commands expressed concerns that State Partnership Program funding would be cut in the future. Bilateral Affairs Officers also expressed similar challenges with funding. For example, one Bilateral Affairs Officer told us that obtaining pay and allowances for guardsmen is difficult compared to active duty forces. Further, three Bilateral Affairs Officers mentioned that they would like to have additional funding to conduct more events and one State Partnership Program Coordinator told us that the National Guard Bureau and the combatant commands do not always have the necessary funds available to support an event.

State Partnership Program Coordinators also expressed concerns about the funding process that extended beyond funding availability. For example, one State Partnership Program Coordinator commented that because funds come from dual sources—the National Guard Bureau and the combatant commands—there is sometimes confusion and funding uncertainties as the two organizations negotiate who will pay for what events or portions of events. Another commented that "the myriad of funding authorizations and their specific peculiarities [are] a challenge to even the most experienced State Partnership Program Coordinator." Further, one State Partnership Program Coordinator told us that because he was not active duty, he did not have access to training offered by the Air Force that he felt would be beneficial to understanding how to better fund events.

The most prominent challenge cited by State Partnership Program stakeholders involved concerns about conducting and funding activities that include civilian participants. In the past, the State Partnership Program has incorporated both U.S. and foreign partner civilians into a variety of activities. These included activities such as subject matter expert exchanges with members of the state's fire department and the host nation on military support to civil authorities; a familiarization on 911 system operations between U.S. and host country civilians; and a subject matter expert exchange with U.S. and foreign partner law enforcement officials on maritime border security issues. However, in response to our question about challenges facing the program, 31 State Partnership Program Coordinators cited difficulties in conducting activities with civilians. In response to our question about how the program should be changed, 36 State Partnership Program Coordinators stated that the program should be changed to better facilitate civilian engagements. Further, many of the State Partnership Program Coordinators expressed the opinion that they were not allowed to conduct activities with civilians at all, even though DOD officials told us that civilians are permitted to participate in activities as long as the proper funding authority is used. For example, one State Partnership Program Coordinator told us that his state's greatest challenge is the current DOD guidance which, based on his understanding, restricts all events to strict military-to-military events. Another State Partnership Program Coordinator told us that the state recently had to cancel planned events with its partner country's civilian authorities because of its interpretation of this guidance. A third State Partnership Program Coordinator stated that the perceived "requirement [to] strictly limit operations to military-to-military engagements limits [the] ability to support" the needs of the embassy and of the partner country. Another State Partnership Program Coordinator told us that the perceived restriction in the DOD guidance prevents his state's capabilities from being fully used.

Bilateral Affairs Officers from the partner country embassies and combatant commands had similar perceptions about civilian participation in State Partnership Program activities. Out of the 23 Bilateral Affairs Officers who provided answers to our questions, 9 cited this area as a challenge for the program. For example, in regard to the challenges posed for the program, one Bilateral Affairs Officer told us that the inability of the National Guard Bureau to bring civilian subject matter experts to the partner countries diminishes the value of events. In addition, 14 of the 23 Bilateral Affairs Officers that responded to our questions expressed the opinion that the State Partnership Program should be changed to better facilitate civilian engagements. For example, one Bilateral Affairs Officer told us that expanding activities into other sectors, such as medical or law enforcement, would help to fulfill embassy and combatant command missions. In addition, one combatant command stated that the restrictions on funding civilians are a challenge facing the program. However, according to DOD officials, the combatant commands have certain funds, such as Traditional Combatant

Commander's Activities funds, which may be available to use for funding events involving civilians.

DOD Has Taken Initial Steps to Clarify Civilian Funding Concerns, but It Is Unclear When Formal Guidance and Training Programs Will Be in Place

DOD has issued some guidance on the State Partnership Program, including guidance on the use of funds for civilians, in part to respond to congressional direction. The National Defense Authorization Act for Fiscal Year 2010 required the Secretary of Defense to prescribe regulations on the use of funds appropriated to DOD to pay the costs incurred by the National Guard in conducting activities under the State Partnership Program, and also required the Secretary to submit annual reports to the appropriate congressional committees describing the civilian engagement activities conducted under the State Partnership Program.[19] In response to the requirement to issue regulations, DOD issued its Directive Type Memorandum in August 2011.[20] The Directive Type Memorandum does not explicitly prohibit the involvement of civilians in State Partnership Program activities; however, it stipulates that funds appropriated to DOD shall not be used to conduct activities with civilians unless those activities are based on legal authority that allows the use of such funds for those activities. National Guard Bureau officials told us that since the issuance of the Directive Type Memorandum, states have become cautious about conducting events with civilians, and many have chosen to not conduct any events with civilians due to a concern about violating DOD guidance. The Directive Type Memorandum will expire in August 2012 and the Under Secretary of Defense, Policy, has drafted an instruction that is intended to further clarify the use of funds appropriated to DOD, including funds for civilian participation, under the State Partnership Program. Officials indicate that this instruction is currently undergoing review within DOD and should be issued sometime during 2012, but could not provide us with a confirmed issuance date. In addition, the National Guard Bureau is working on guidance for implementing the State Partnership Program. According to National Guard Bureau officials, an instruction will establish policy, assign responsibilities, and provide guidance for the execution of the State Partnership Program. An accompanying manual will provide more details on how to implement the program. National Guard Bureau officials indicated that the instruction and the manual are expected to be

---

[19]Pub. L. No 111-84, § 1210 (2009).

[20]Under Secretary of Defense, Policy Directive Type Memorandum, Directive-Type Memorandum (DTM) 11-010, *"Use of Appropriated Funds for Conducting State Partnership Program (SPP) Activities"* (Aug. 19, 2011).

issued sometime during 2012, but also could not provide us with a confirmed issuance date.

During the course of our review, Congress enacted the National Defense Authorization Act for Fiscal Year 2012, which provides authority for the use of up to $3 million to pay for some costs associated with civilian participation.[21] However, National Guard Bureau officials stated that DOD has not issued guidance on the implementation of this provision. According to officials, due to this lack of guidance, funds have not been used for this purpose. The draft DOD instruction is still undergoing review and is intended to provide clarifying information on the use of funds appropriated to DOD prior to the enactment of the National Defense Authorization Act for Fiscal Year 2012. Therefore, it may be appropriate for the Under Secretary of Defense, Policy, to determine whether or not the draft instruction is the right mechanism for conveying additional guidance addressing section 1085 of the National Defense Authorization Act for Fiscal Year 2012, or determine alternative plans for how to address the confusion expressed by National Guard Bureau officials. Without additional guidance, however, the National Guard Bureau does not plan to use this authority so the concerns about how to fund civilian participation are likely to persist.

Beyond the lack of guidance, the responses stakeholders provided to our questions revealed that there is widespread confusion about aspects of program implementation, including addressing funding concerns. We have previously reported that challenges facing such programs can be mitigated by improving training and that training can help ensure that program policies and procedures are consistently adhered to by program

---

[21]Section 1085 of the National Defense Authorization Act for Fiscal Year 2012, Pub. L. No. 112-81 (2011), allows the Secretary of Defense to use up to $3,000,000 of the funds made available to the National Guard to pay for travel and per diem costs associated with the participation of the United States and foreign civilian and non-defense agency personnel in conducting activities under the State Partnership Program of the National Guard, subject to Section 1210 of the National Defense Authorization Act for Fiscal Year 2010, Pub. L. No. 111–84 (2009), codified at 32 U.S.C. 107 note. Section 1210 of the National Defense Authorization Act for Fiscal Year 2010 states that funds shall not be available for activities conducted under the State Partnership Program in a foreign country unless such activities are jointly approved by the commander of the combatant command and the chief of mission concerned.

offices.[22] Further, DOD guidance emphasizes the need for proper training and staffing to increase effectiveness in budgeting.[23] The National Guard Bureau has taken steps to provide training but told us that their efforts needed improvement in some areas. For example, State Partnership Program Coordinators have the opportunity to attend the Defense Institute of Security Assistance Management course, which in 2012 and several years prior, included topics such as an introduction to security cooperation, understanding the State Partnership Program, emphasizing security cooperation administration as well as emphasizing the interaction and constraints of the State Partnership Program with other DOD security cooperation activities. Moreover, officials indicated that the National Guard Bureau holds annual State Partnership Program conferences and participates in combatant commands' conferences, where some training on the processes and authorities are presented. National Guard Bureau officials stated that they are planning some training for State Partnership Program Coordinators for the summer of 2012 and plan to include an overview of funding, but have not determined the specific content related to funding for this training event. Without further guidance and training in this area, the National Guard Bureau and the combatant commands may miss additional opportunities to use the program to fulfill their missions.

Conclusions

In recent years, DOD has emphasized the importance of strengthening security cooperation with other countries as a way of promoting stability and partner capacity around the world, and the State Partnership Program is one of many efforts in this area. While many State Partnership Program stakeholders cited anecdotal benefits to the program such as training and experience for guardsmen and supporting combatant commanders' goals and priorities, DOD and Congress do not have an effective means to assess the program because fundamental elements such as agreed-upon goals are missing. As a result, little oversight of the program has been conducted in the past. Officials informed us that they are working on goals, objectives, and metrics and expect to implement them in the next few months. Such goals and measures are critical because they form the foundation of an oversight framework that would

---

[22]GAO, *Indian Health Service: Increased Oversight Needed to Ensure Accuracy of Data Used for Estimating Contract Health Service Need*, GAO-11-767 (Washington, D.C.: Sept. 23, 2011).

[23]Joint Publication 1-04, *Legal Support to Military Operations* (Mar. 1, 2007).

enable decision makers and stakeholders to objectively judge the program's effectiveness and gauge progress over time. However, in order to make use of metrics, DOD and the National Guard Bureau will need complete and consistent data from the combatant commands and state National Guards engaged in State Partnership Program activities. In the interim period until DOD fully implements its global data system, guidance that establishes an agreed-upon set of definitions and rules for inputting data, and that would apply to the National Guard Bureau, all combatant commands, and state National Guards, could provide a foundation for measuring the State Partnership Program's effectiveness and efficiency. Finally, some activities that stakeholders believe could have a broad impact—such as those involving civilians—are not being conducted due primarily to a lack of guidance and understanding on how to fund those activities. Ensuring that stakeholders understand how to use funding from the National Guard Bureau, combatant commands, and other sources to support the State Partnership Program would help state National Guards fully utilize the program.

Recommendations for Executive Action

We recommend that the Secretary of Defense take the following four actions:

- To improve the management of the State Partnership Program, direct the Chief of the National Guard Bureau, in coordination with the combatant commands and the embassy country teams, to complete and implement the program's comprehensive oversight framework by using the goals, objectives, and metrics currently being developed as its basis.
- To enable oversight and improve the completeness and consistency of data needed to manage the State Partnership Program, direct the Under Secretary of Defense for Policy and Joint Staff, in coordination with the Chief of the National Guard Bureau, the combatant commands, and the embassy country teams, to develop guidance for all stakeholders that includes agreed-upon definitions for data fields and rules for maintaining data until the global data system is fully implemented.
- To address concerns about how funds can be used to include civilians in State Partnership Program activities, direct the Under Secretary of Defense for Policy, to develop guidance that clarifies how to use funds for civilian participation in the State Partnership Program.
- To improve program implementation, direct the Chief of the National Guard Bureau to develop additional training for State Partnership Program Coordinators and Bilateral Affairs Officers on the appropriate

use of funds for supporting the State Partnership Program, especially in regard to including civilians in program events.

Agency Comments and Our Evaluation

In written comments on a draft of this report, DOD concurred with our findings and recommendations. Regarding our first recommendation to complete and implement the program's comprehensive oversight framework, DOD concurred and noted that these efforts are underway with target implementation for the end of fiscal year 2012. In response to our second recommendation to develop guidance for all stakeholders that includes agreed-upon definitions for data fields and rules for maintaining data, and our third recommendation to develop guidance that clarifies the use of funds for civilian participation in State Partnership Program activities, DOD concurred and stated that it is currently developing a DOD instruction that will provide additional guidance to stakeholders on these issues. DOD did not, however, indicate timelines for the issuance of this instruction. We believe that prompt action in this regard will help DOD achieve greater visibility over the State Partnership Program, and we urge DOD to determine a timeline for issuance. Regarding our final recommendation to develop additional training for State Partnership Program Coordinators and Bilateral Affairs Officers on the appropriate use of funds for supporting the State Partnership Program, especially in regard to including civilians in program events, DOD concurred and stated that the National Guard Bureau has developed some additional training and will use existing workshops to increase training opportunities. We are pleased with DOD's efforts and continue to believe that increased training in this area will help DOD fully utilize the State Partnership Program. DOD's comments are printed in their entirety in appendix III.

We also provided a draft of this report to the Department of State and the United States Agency for International Development, but they did not provide any comments.

We are sending copies of this report to appropriate congressional committees, the Secretary of Defense, the Secretary of State, and the Administrator of the United States Agency for International Development. This report is also available at no charge on the GAO website at http://www.gao.gov.

If you or your staff have any questions regarding this report, please contact me at (202) 512-3489 or pendletonj@gao.gov. Contact points for our Offices of Congressional Relations and Public Affairs may be found on the last page of this report. GAO staff who made key contributions to this report are listed in appendix IV.

John H. Pendleton
Director, Defense Capabilities and Management

Appendix I: Scope and Methodology

To address our objectives, we collected perspectives on the program from the Office of the Secretary of Defense, Policy; Joint Staff; National Guard Bureau; and program stakeholders including State Partnership Program coordinating officials at the geographic combatant commands; State Partnership Program Coordinators; and Bilateral Affairs Officers, including their views on the benefits of the program. We also collected information on the process that the Department of Defense (DOD) uses to establish partnerships and the steps taken by all U.S. program stakeholders, including State Partnership Program Coordinators, Bilateral Affairs Officers, and combatant commanders, to coordinate State Partnership Program activities and prevent duplication of effort. We also obtained and reviewed DOD documents, including Defense Strategic Guidance, the Quadrennial Defense Review, and The National Military Strategy of the United States of America to place the State Partnership Program within the broader context of DOD's strategic efforts.

To determine the extent to which State Partnership Program activities are meeting the goals and objectives of the program, we gathered documentation; interviewed National Guard Bureau officials about the development of goals, objectives, and performance metrics for the program; and assessed their efforts based on criteria from our previous work. We also reviewed an improvement plan for the State Partnership Program provided by the National Guard Bureau and assessed the extent to which the plan addressed the need for goals, objectives, and metrics and identified timeframes for implementation. In addition, we obtained and reviewed DOD guidance, including the Directive Type Memorandum released in August 2011, to determine if goals and objectives for the State Partnership Program were specified in those documents. To identify benefits of the program, we contacted all State Partnership Program Coordinators and Bilateral Affairs Officers via e-mail with a standard set of questions. In addition to program benefits, the questions addressed roles in implementing the State Partnership Program, steps to avoid duplication of program activities, any challenges faced when implementing the program, and any suggested areas for improvement. We received and analyzed responses from 50 of the 52 State Partnership Program Coordinators and from 23 out of 47 Bilateral Affairs Officers.[1] We also collected and analyzed written responses to similar questions

---

[1]There are 53 U.S. states and territories currently participating in the State Partnership Program. While there are 63 partnerships in the program, not every country has a Bilateral Affairs Officer assigned.

from coordinating officials at the six U.S. geographic combatant commands.

In conducting our content analysis, a GAO analyst independently reviewed each response from the State Partnership Program Coordinators and Bilateral Affairs Officers to identify recurring themes in the answers to each question. A second GAO analyst independently reviewed the responses from the State Partnership Program Coordinators and Bilateral Affairs Officers and reviewed the recurring themes identified by the first analyst to reach concurrence and identify any themes that the first analyst may have overlooked. Using the identified recurring themes, the analysts developed categories and definitions for what should and should not be included under each category when coding the responses. A GAO analyst then independently reviewed the answers to each question and placed them into one or more of the relevant categories. In some cases, the respondent may have provided information to answer the question in other areas of the response. When that occurred, the analyst also coded that information and noted that it was provided in an answer to a different question. A second GAO analyst independently reviewed the answers to each question and placed them into one or more of the relevant categories. The coding of both analysts was compared to identify areas of disagreement. For items in which there was not agreement, the two analysts met to discuss reasons for selecting the categories they did until an agreement about the category that was most appropriate was reached.

To determine the completeness and consistency of activity and funding data for the program, we collected and analyzed data on State Partnership Program activities from fiscal years 2007 through 2011—including types of activities, funding sources, and funding amounts—obtained from the National Guard Bureau and the six U.S. geographic combatant commands. To assess the reliability of the data, we collected written information from the combatant commands to gain an understanding of the processes and databases used to collect and record data and to identify any known limitations to the data. We also collected written information on any data quality control procedures in place for data on State Partnership Program activities and reviewed user manuals for the various databases, where provided. We discussed the procedures for generating and verifying the data with knowledgeable combatant command and National Guard Bureau officials. We examined the data provided for obvious anomalies and compared the data to DOD's report to Congress on State Partnership Program activities involving civilians. We found missing information and inconsistencies as well as a lack of guidance on data inputs to ensure complete and consistent information. We discussed these limitations with the officials in an attempt to obtain more complete information and reconcile the differences. We ultimately determined that the data we received were not reliable for the purposes of providing complete information on the types and frequency of activities, the funding sources used, or the total cost of the activities because of our concerns about the completeness and consistency of the data, which we discuss in our report. As a result, the data we included in the report do not represent the complete scope of the State Partnership Program. The data do, however, illustrate the limitations we found.

To identify challenges that DOD faces in implementing the program, we included a question on any challenges in implementing the program and any areas for improvement in our email to all State Partnership Program Coordinators and all Bilateral Affairs Officers who participate in this program, as described above. Our content analysis included categories for challenges and areas for improvement. We also collected and analyzed written responses to similar questions from the six U.S. geographic combatant commands. On the basis of the challenges cited by stakeholders, we also reviewed legislation and guidance on the State Partnership Program, including the Directive Type Memorandum and internal National Guard Bureau memoranda on the use of funds for State Partnership Program activities, to identify areas of confusion that might require clarification or additional training. We also identified criteria in our previous work for combating the challenges identified by State Partnership Program stakeholders. We discussed these areas with National Guard Bureau officials and any efforts in place to address the challenges.

We conducted this performance audit from August 2011 to May 2012 in accordance with generally accepted government auditing standards. Those standards require that we plan and perform the audit to obtain sufficient, appropriate evidence to provide a reasonable basis for our findings and conclusions based on our audit objectives. We believe that the evidence obtained provides a reasonable basis for our findings and conclusions based on our audit objectives.

Figure 4: State Partnership Program Participating States and Countries, Africa Command

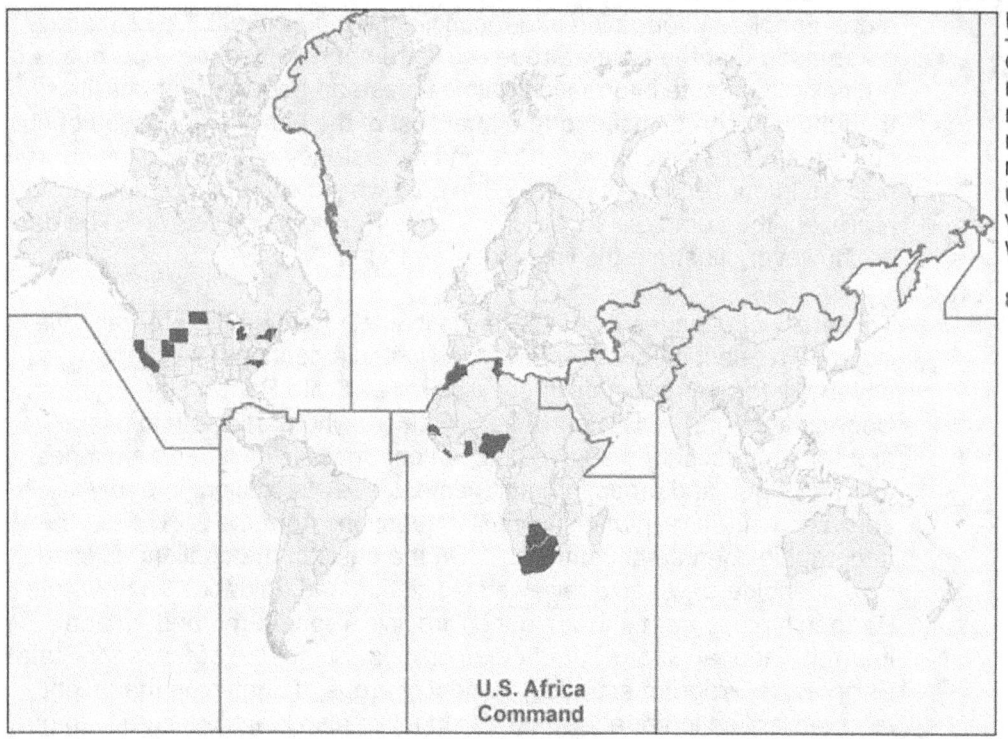

U.S. Africa Command

California and Nigeria* (2006)
New York and South Africa* (2003)
North Carolina and Botswana* (2008)
North Dakota and Ghana* (2004)
Michigan and Liberia* (2009)
Utah and Morocco* (2003)
Vermont and Senegal* (2008)
Wyoming and Tunisia* (2004)

8 partnerships

U.S. Africa Command

Source: National Guard Bureau.
*Indicates country has a Bilateral Affairs Officer.

Figure 5: State Partnership Program Participating States and Countries, Central Command

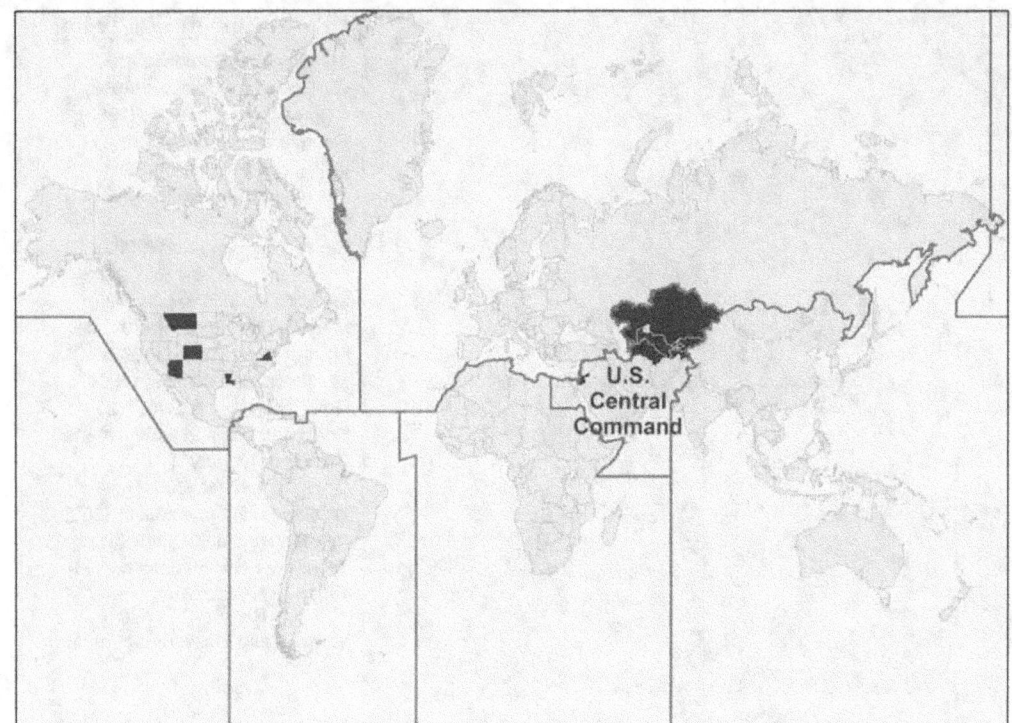

U.S. Central Command

Arizona and Kazakhstan (1993)
Colorado and Jordan (2004)
Louisiana and Uzbekistan (1996)
Montana and Kyrgyzstan (1996)
Virginia and Tajikistan (2003)
Pending and Turkmenistan (1996)

6 partnerships

Source: National Guard Bureau.

Figure 6: State Partnership Program Participating States and Countries, European Command

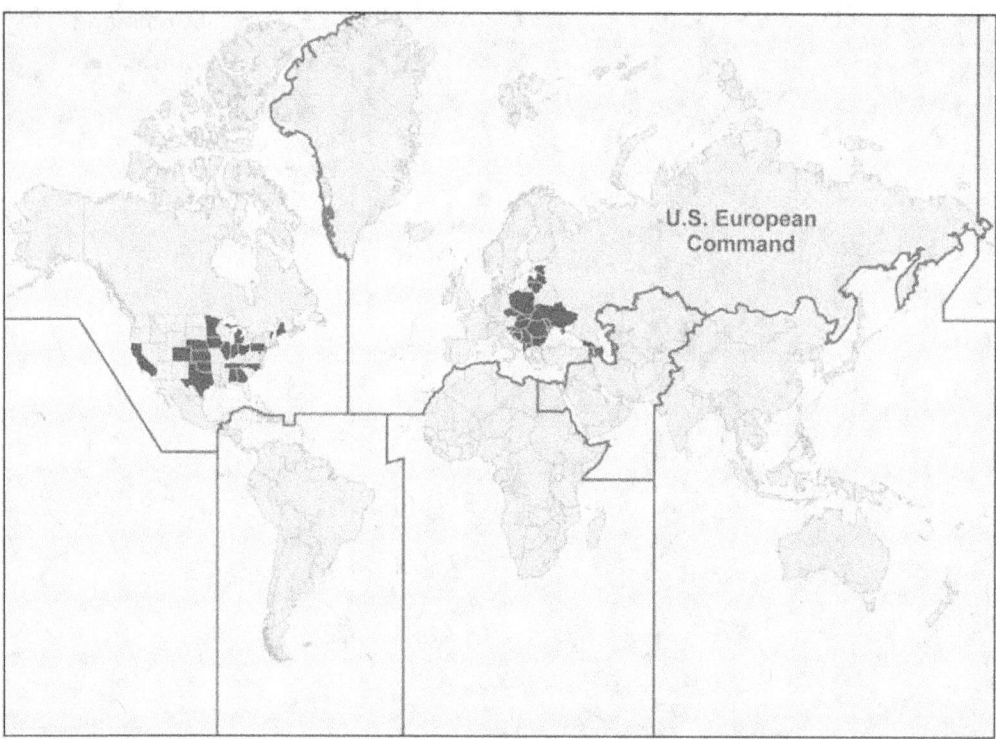

U.S. European Command

Alabama and Romania* (1993)
California and Ukraine* (1993)
Colorado and Slovenia* (1993)
Georgia and Georgia* (1994)
Illinois and Poland* (1993)
Indiana and Slovakia* (1993)
Iowa and Kosovo* (2011)
Kansas and Armenia* (2002)
Maine and Montenegro* (2006)
Maryland and Estonia* (1993)
Maryland and Bosnia* (2003)
Michigan and Latvia* (1993)
Minnesota and Croatia* (1996)
New Jersey and Albania* (2001)
North Carolina and Moldova* (1996)
Ohio and Hungary* (1993)
Ohio and Serbia* (2005)
Oklahoma and Azerbaijan* (2002)
Pennsylvania and Lithuania* (1993)
Tennessee and Bulgaria* (1993)
Texas / Nebraska and
    Czech Republic* (1993)
Vermont and Macedonia* (1993)

22 partnerships

Source: National Guard Bureau.
*Indicates country has a Bilateral Affairs Officer.

Figure 7: State Partnership Program Participating States and Countries, Northern Command

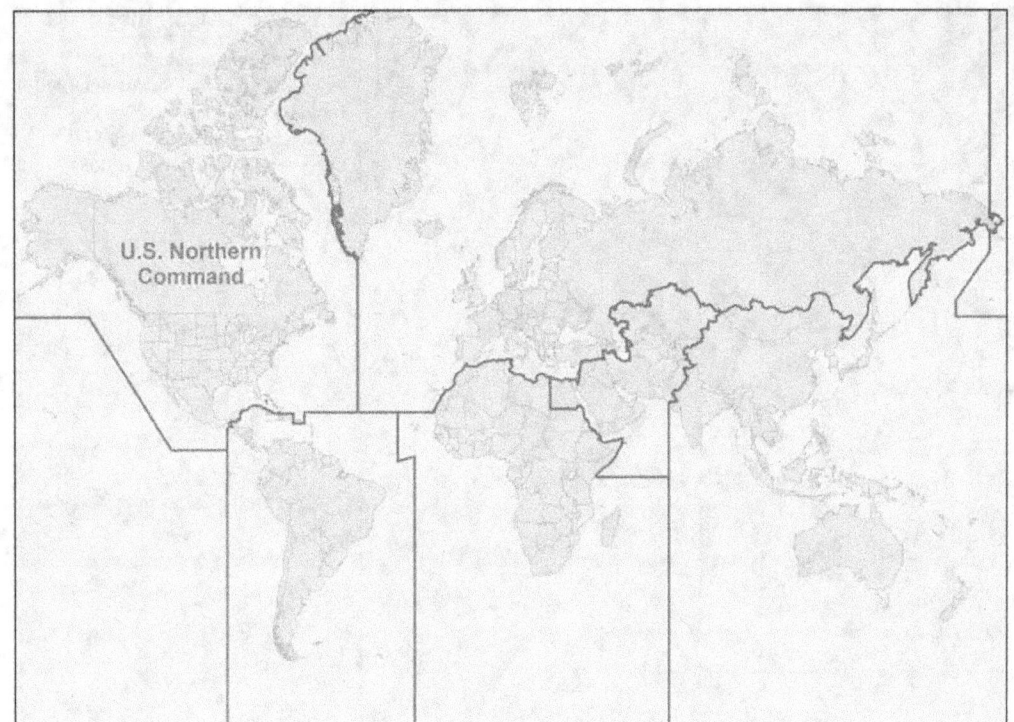

U.S. Northern Command

Rhode Island and Bahamas (2005)

1 partnership

Source: National Guard Bureau.

Figure 8: State Partnership Program Participating States and Countries, Pacific Command

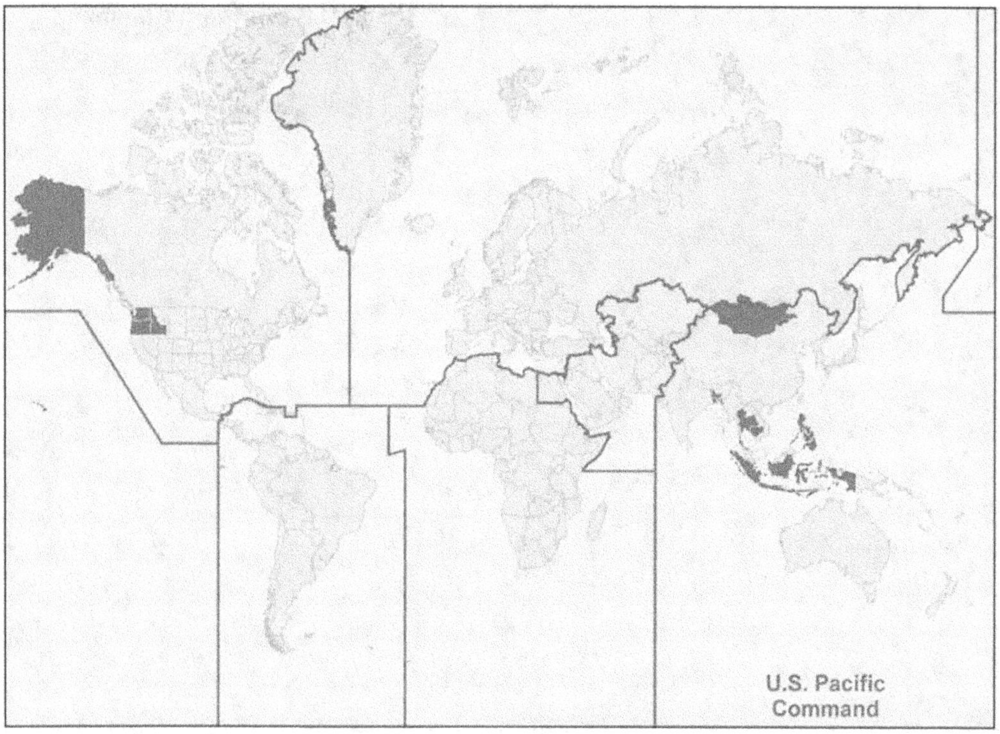

U.S. Pacific Command

Alaska and Mongolia (2003)
Hawaii / Guam and Philippines (2000)
Hawaii and Indonesia (2006)
Idaho and Cambodia (2009)
Oregon and Bangladesh (2008)
Washington and Thailand (2002)

6 partnerships

U.S. Pacific
Command

Source: National Guard Bureau.

Figure 9: State Partnership Program Participating States and Countries, Southern Command

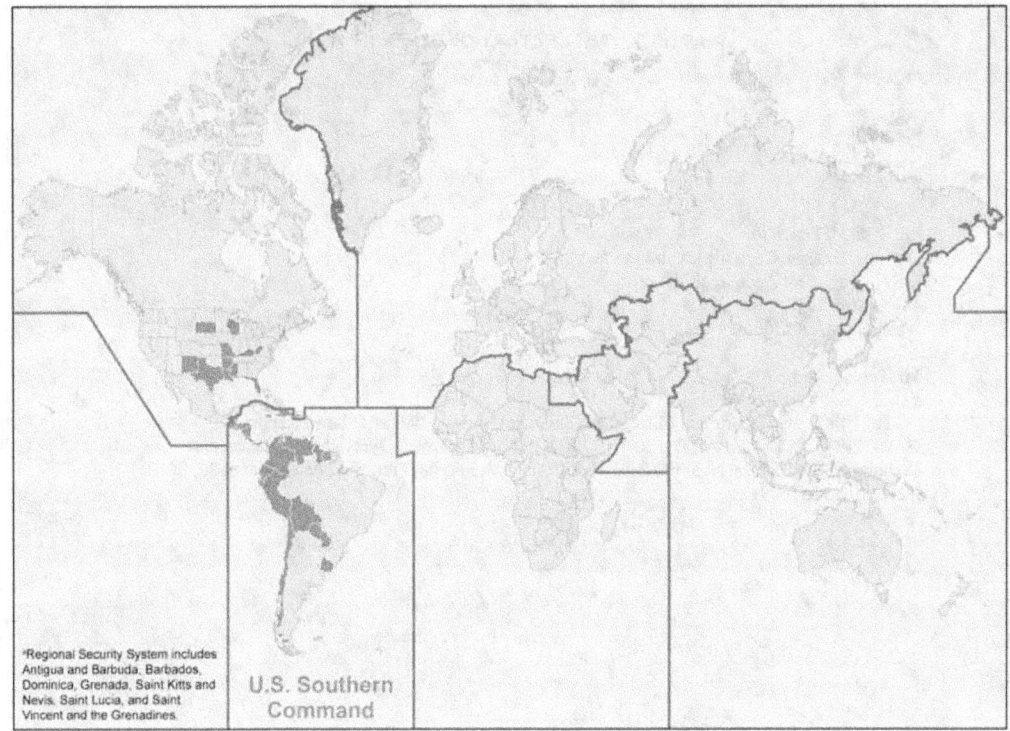

U.S. Southern Command

Arkansas and Guatemala (2002)
Connecticut and Uruguay* (2000)
Delaware and Trinidad-Tobago* (2004)
District of Columbia and
  Jamaica* (1999)
Florida and Venezuela (1998)
Florida and Guyana* (2003)
Florida/Virgin Islands with
  Regional Security System[a]* (2006)
Kentucky and Ecuador* (1996)
Louisiana and Belize* (1996)
Louisiana and Haiti* (2011)
Massachusetts and Paraguay* (2001)
Mississippi and Bolivia (1999)
Missouri and Panama* (1996)
New Hampshire and
  El Salvador* (2000)
New Mexico and Costa Rica* (2006)
Puerto Rico and Honduras* (1998)
Puerto Rico and Dominican
  Republic* (2003)
South Dakota and Suriname* (2006)
Texas and Chile* (2008)
West Virginia and Peru* (1996)
Wisconsin and Nicaragua* (2003)
Pending and Colombia (2012)

22 partnerships

ªRegional Security System includes
Antigua and Barbuda, Barbados,
Dominica, Grenada, Saint Kitts and
Nevis, Saint Lucia, and Saint
Vincent and the Grenadines.

U.S. Southern
Command

Source: National Guard Bureau.
*Indicates country has a Bilateral Affairs Officer.

Appendix III: Comments from the Department of Defense

Note: GAO received
DOD's letter
April 27, 2012

ASSISTANT SECRETARY OF DEFENSE
2500 DEFENSE PENTAGON
WASHINGTON, D.C. 20301-2500

SPECIAL OPERATIONS/
LOW-INTENSITY CONFLICT

Mr. John H. Pendleton
Director, Defense Capabilities and Management
U.S. Government Accountability Office
441 G Street, NW
Washington, DC 20548

Mr. Pendleton:

This is the Department of Defense (DoD) response to the GAO Draft Report, GAO-12-548, "STATE PARTNERSHIP PROGRAM: Improved Oversight, Guidance, and Training Needed for the National Guard's Efforts with Foreign Partners," dated March 30, 2012 (GAO Code 351649).

Sincerely,

Michael A. Sheehan

GAO DRAFT REPORT DATED MARCH 30, 2012
GAO-12-548 (GAO CODE 351649)

"STATE PARTNERSHIP PROGRAM: IMPROVED OVERSIGHT, GUIDANCE, AND TRAINING NEEDED FOR NATIONAL GUARD'S EFFORTS WITH FOREIGN PARTNERS"

DEPARTMENT OF DEFENSE COMMENTS
TO THE GAO RECOMMENDATIONS

RECOMMENDATION 1: The GAO recommends that the Secretary of Defense direct the Chief of the National Guard Bureau, in coordination with the combatant commands and the embassy country teams, to complete and implement its comprehensive oversight framework by using the goals, objectives, and metrics currently being developed as its basis.

DoD RESPONSE: DoD concurs. As reported in the study, the National Guard Bureau acknowledges the need for updated program goals and objectives to more accurately reflect the current operating environment and the need for development of metrics to measure and assess program progress. Both of these efforts to update the oversight framework are well underway and will be incorporated into updates to the National Guard Bureau's policy and strategy documents for the State Partnership Program. Distribution to the States and implementing instructions are targeted for the end of this fiscal year.

RECOMMENDATION 2: The GAO recommends that the Secretary of Defense direct the Under Secretary of Defense, Policy, and Joint Staff, in coordination with Chief of the National Guard Bureau, the combatant commands, and the embassy country teams, to develop guidance for all stakeholders that includes agreed-upon definitions for data fields and rules for maintaining data until the global data system is fully implemented.

DoD RESPONSE: DoD concurs. The Department is currently writing a Department of Defense Instruction (DoDI) which will replace the current Directive Type Memorandum (DTM) 11-011, "Use of Appropriated Funds for Conducting State Partnership Program (SPP) Activities". This DoDI will provide additional guidance to all stakeholders that will include the issues indentified in this GAO report.

RECOMMENDATION 3: The GAO recommends that the Secretary of Defense direct the Under Secretary of Defense, Policy, to develop guidance that clarifies how to use funds for civilian participation in the State Partnership Program.

DoD RESPONSE: DoD concurs. The Department is currently writing a Department of Defense Instruction (DoDI) which will replace the current Directive Type Memorandum

(DTM) 11-011, "Use of Appropriated Funds for Conducting State Partnership Program
(SPP) Activities". This DoDI will provide additional guidance to all stakeholders that
will include the issues indentified in this GAO report.

RECOMMENDATION 4: The GAO recommends that the Secretary of Defense direct
the Chief of the National Guard Bureau to develop additional training for State
Partnership Program Coordinators and Bilateral Affairs Officers on the appropriate use of
funds for supporting the State Partnership Program, especially in regards to including
civilians in program events.

DoD RESPONSE: DoD concurs. The National Guard Bureau currently uses various
forums for the training of State Partnership Program stakeholders to include dedicated
courses at the Defense Institute of Security Assistance Management (DISAM),
Combatant Command Regional Workshops, and National Guard Bureau Workshops.
The National Guard Bureau recognizes the need for emphasis on training to ensure
adherence to program policies and procedures. To that end, the National Guard Bureau
has developed additional DISAM curricula relevant to State Partnership Program
Coordinators and Bilateral Affairs Officers, and will use existing workshops and State
Coordinators' monthly VTCs to increase training opportunities.

Appendix IV: GAO Contact and Staff Acknowledgments

GAO Contact

John H. Pendleton, (202) 512-3489 or pendletonj@gao.gov

Staff Acknowledgments

In addition to the contact named above, key contributors to this report were Marie Mak, Assistant Director; Leslie Bharadwaja; Michele Fejfar; Kelly Liptan; Erik Wilkins-McKee; Amie Steele; and Nicole Willems.

www.ingramcontent.com/pod-product-compliance
Lightning Source LLC
Chambersburg PA
CBHW080921290526
45795CB00007BA/2601

9781492101949